Titles in this series
Hal the Hero
The Little Queen

First published in 1999 by
Wayland Publishers Ltd
61 Western Road, Hove
East Sussex BN3 1JD, England

Text copyright © Stewart Ross 1999

Stewart Ross and Sue Shields have asserted their moral right to be identified as the author and illustrator of this work respectively, in accordance with the Copyright, Designs and Patents Act, 1988.

Series editor: Alex Woolf
Book designer: Jean Wheeler

British Library Cataloguing in Publication Data
Ross, Stewart
Hal the hero : the amazing story of King Henry VIII. - (Stories from history)
1.Henry, VIII, King of England - Juvenile literature
2.Great Britain - Kings and rulers - Biography - Juvenile literature 3.Great Britain - History - Henry VIII, 1509-1547 - Juvenile literature
I.Title
942'.052'092

ISBN 0 7502 2499 1

Typeset by Jean Wheeler
Printed and bound in Portugal by Edições ASA

Hal the Hero

Stewart Ross
Illustrated by Sue Shields

WAYLAND

This is the sad story of a king called Henry.

Henry was young and handsome.

He was sporty and clever.

Everyone liked him.

But King Henry was very spoilt.

His friends spoilt him,

and his soldiers spoilt him.

The ladies spoilt him.

Henry grew proud and fat and grumpy,

and things started to go wrong.

Henry had a great ship called the Mary Rose.

The Mary Rose turned over and sank.

Henry went to war.

Many soldiers died.

Some people did not like Henry now.

Henry took money from the church.

Henry did not have many friends.

Henry married six times.

Two wives did not love him.

Henry cut off their heads.

The King grew fatter and fatter,

and grumpier and grumpier.

At last King Henry died. A few people cried ...

Do you know?

This story is TRUE!
The king is called HENRY THE EIGHTH.
This is also written 'Henry VIII'.
Henry was King of England 500 years ago.
This is what he looked like when he was a young man:

Notes for adults

Hal the Hero and the National Curriculum.

Hal the Hero grew out of the ideas presented in two recent documents: the Department for Education and Employment's *National Literacy Strategy* and the Qualifications and Curriculum Authority's *Maintaining Breadth and Balance at Key Stages 1 and 2*. It is both a Key Stage 1 reader, offering stimulating material for use during the Literacy Hour, and a useful springboard for Key Stage 1 history. In presenting the story of Henry VIII in the simplest possible terms, it introduces the child to one of the best-known figures from British history, and presents many opportunities for (a) 'looking for similarities and differences between life today and in the past', (b) 'talking and writing about what happened and why people acted as they did', and (c) 'finding out about the past using different sources of information and representations'. (*Maintaining Breadth and Balance*, p. 10.)

Suggested follow-up activities

1. Checking the child knows and can use words they might not have come across before. In particular:

hero	handsome	sporty	clever
brave	spoilt	grumble	grumpy
soldier	church	everyone	people
married	wives	hooray	hurrah
ship	sank	hello	wrong

2. Talking about things remaining from Henry's time, e.g. buildings (Hampton Court and much domestic architecture), the *Mary Rose*, the portrait of the King (opposite), etc.

3. Discussing how we know about Henry VIII, i.e. sources (perhaps starting with the portrait).

4. Explaining the exact dates of Henry's reign (1509-1547) and what they mean.

5. Going further into aspects of Henry's reign, e.g. his marriages (the names of his wives and why he needed a male heir), his wars (several of his coastal forts remain intact), and his attack on the church (are there monastic ruins nearby?).

6. Comparing life in Henry's time with our own, e.g. executions, clothing, sailing ships.